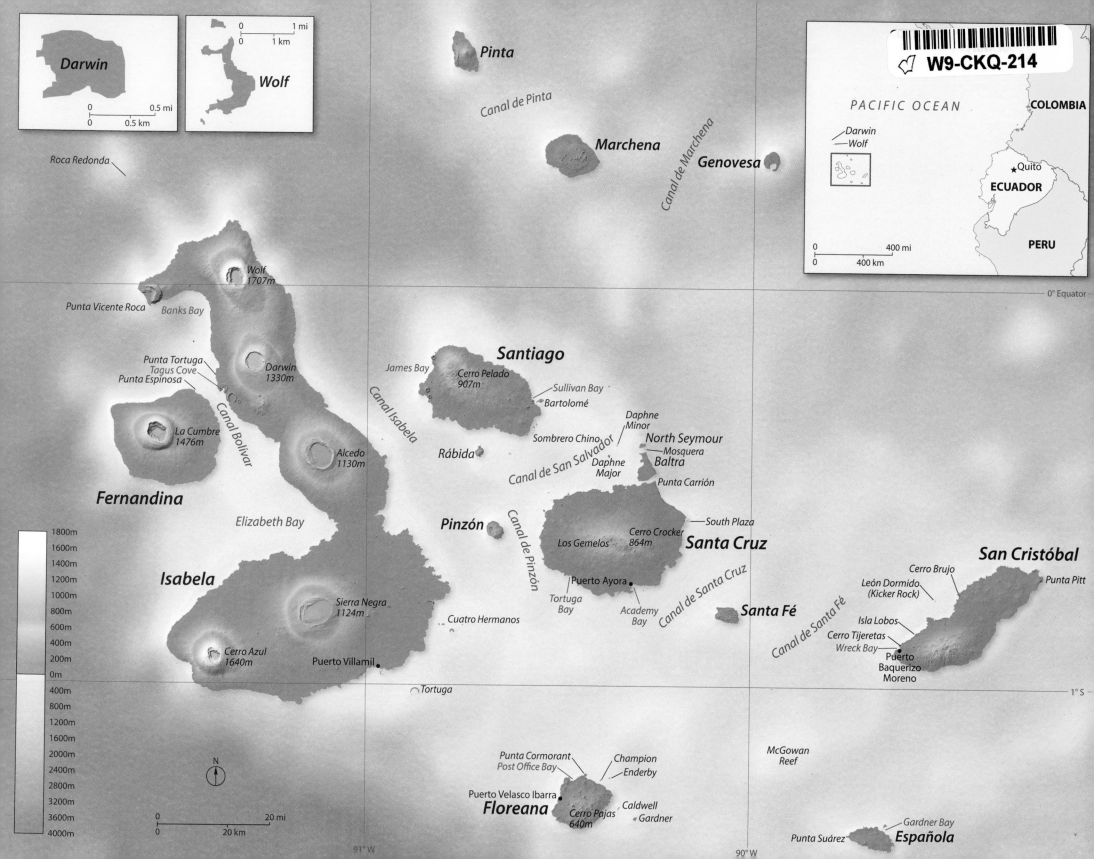

Darwin

0   0.5 mi
0   0.5 km

0   1 mi
0   1 km

Wolf

W9-CKQ-214

PACIFIC OCEAN   **COLOMBIA**

Darwin
Wolf

★Quito

ECUADOR

PERU

0   400 mi
0   400 km

Roca Redonda

Pinta

Canal de Pinta

Marchena

Canal de Marchena

Genovesa

0° Equator

Wolf
1707m

Punta Vicente Roca   *Banks Bay*

Punta Tortuga
Tagus Cove
Punta Espinosa

Darwin
1330m

Santiago

James Bay

Cerro Pelado
907m

Sullivan Bay

Bartolomé

La Cumbre
1476m

Canal Bolívar

Alcedo
1130m

Canal Isabela

Sombrero Chino

Daphne
Minor

North Seymour

Rábida

Canal de San Salvador

Daphne
Major

Mosquera
Baltra

Fernandina

Elizabeth Bay

Punta Carrión

South Plaza

Pinzón

Canal de Pinzón

Cerro Crocker
864m

Los Gemelos

Santa Cruz

San Cristóbal

Cerro Brujo

Punta Pitt

Isabela

Sierra Negra
1124m

Puerto Ayora

Canal de Santa Cruz

Santa Fé

León Dormido
(Kicker Rock)

Isla Lobos

Cerro Azul
1640m

Cuatro Hermanos

Tortuga
Bay

Academy
Bay

Canal de Santa Fé

Cerro Tijeretas

Wreck Bay

Puerto Villamil

Puerto
Baquerizo
Moreno

Tortuga

1° S

McGowan
Reef

Punta Cormorant
Post Office Bay

Champion
Enderby

Puerto Velasco Ibarra

Caldwell

Floreana

Cerro Pajas
640m

Gardner

Gardner Bay

Punta Suárez

Española

1800m
1600m
1400m
1200m
1000m
800m
600m
400m
200m
0m
400m
800m
1200m
1600m
2000m
2400m
2800m
3200m
3600m
4000m

N

0   20 mi
0   20 km

91° W

90° W

GALÁPAGOS

Three **BLUE-FOOTED BOOBIES** perched on a cliff with a **SWALLOW-TAILED GULL** flying by, Gardner Islet

GALÁPAGOS

Life in Motion

WALTER PEREZ & MICHAEL WEISBERG

PRINCETON UNIVERSITY PRESS

PRINCETON AND OXFORD

Photographs copyright © 2018 Walter Perez

Text copyright © 2018 Michael Weisberg and Walter Perez

Requests for permission to reproduce material from this work should
be sent to Permissions, Princeton University Press

Published by Princeton University Press,
41 William Street, Princeton, New Jersey 08540

In the United Kingdom: Princeton University Press,
6 Oxford Street, Woodstock, Oxfordshire OX20 1TR

press.princeton.edu

Jacket photo by Walter Perez

Jacket design by Lorraine Betz Doneker

Photograph opposite: Short-eared Owl ready to hunt, Genovesa Island

All Rights Reserved

ISBN 978-0-691-17413-6

Library of Congress Control Number: 2018932162

British Library Cataloging-in-Publication Data is available

This book has been composed in Proxima Nova

Printed on acid-free paper. ∞

Designed by D & N Publishing, Baydon, Wiltshire, UK

Printed in China

10 9 8 7 6 5 4 3 2 1

DEDICATIONS

FOR MY PARENTS, JUAN PÉREZ AND MARIANA OJEDA,
WHO ENCOURAGED ME TO FOLLOW MY DREAMS

WP

FOR BRANDON

MW

CONTENTS

ESPAÑOLA MOCKINGBIRDS fighting
over territory, Española Island

"THE ARCHIPELAGO IS A LITTLE WORLD WITHIN ITSELF ..."

Charles Darwin, *The Voyage of the Beagle*, 1839

The Galápagos archipelago is a series of 330 volcanic islands, islets, and smaller rocks located 620 nautical miles off the coast of mainland Ecuador. This barren place in the middle of the East Pacific Ocean is more like a desert than a tropical paradise. Water is always scarce, so plants and animals need to conserve it or find a way to desalinate seawater. Food is often scarce as well, so animals need to specialize in eating something abundant, or they must become generalists. Populations are small, so finding a good mate is a challenge. In fact, every moment of survival is a challenge, making these islands one of the best places to study evolution in action.

For those interested in wildlife, the Galápagos fauna offers an extraordinary opportunity to get up close and personal. These animals are, for the most part, ecologically naïve. They evolved in an environment without many large predators, and they tend to ignore humans. But although it is possible to observe many Galápagos animals easily, to really understand what is happening in this place, it is necessary to come back again and again, re-observing animal behaviors under different circumstances and in different seasons. This is not easy for the occasional visitor.

Luckily for the rest of us, Walter Perez has spent most of his adult life studying and photographing these extraordinary animals. The pictures in this book are the result of a dozen years of close study with a camera, organized to illustrate how Galápagos animals manage to live—from the bottom of the ocean to the tops of the trees. In these pages, we will see a wide assortment of animals building a home, finding food, attracting mates, and raising their young. These photos will show them defending their territories, sharing tender moments with their partners, and displaying remarkable adaptations to living in one of the most extraordinary places on the planet.

Although the astonishing images in this book were taken with one man's camera, they were made possible by many friends and colleagues.

Walter says:
There simply isn't enough space to list all the people who have played an important role in my life and who have helped me become who I am since I came to the Galápagos as a young adult. I want to thank all my colleagues on the *National Geographic Endeavor* and the *National Geographic Islander* for ten years of working together, for your friendship, and for the time spent chatting, dancing, laughing, and learning. Thanks to all the crew members for your respect and friendship and the wonderful, vivid moments in the Galápagos. I also thank Bob Young for planting a seed in my head and teaching me that a big project is possible with work and perseverance, and Michael Weisberg for accepting my idea and helping me put my thoughts into motion, turning this project from a dream into a reality. I owe a special debt to Evelyn Faulkner for her friendship and non-ending support during this laborious process. And last but not least, a special thank-you is due to all the National Geographic and Lindblad Expeditions photographers for sharing your amazing skills during every photo workshop and expedition.

Michael says:
My life and work have been enriched by the time I have spent in the Galápagos, getting to know its flora, its fauna, and most importantly, its people. Without Walter, this book would not have been possible—I am grateful for his partnership. I am also especially grateful for the friendship of Ernesto Vaca and Fausto Rodriguez, who are tremendous guides, natural-born leaders, and wonderful people. I have also been privileged to work with many other Naturalist Guides and Galápagos National Park officials, so thanks to them for their support, assistance, and friendship. Thanks also to Jack Gove and Irby Lovette for their assistance on complex matters of nomenclature. My community engagement and cinematic projects in the archipelago, part of the inspiration for this book, would not have been possible without Mike Attie, Elysia Choi, Brian Christiansen, Sabrina Elkassas, SR Foxley, Carla Hoge, Kelly Kennedy, Karen Kovaka, Emelen Metz, Maddie Tilyou, and Justin Walsh. I have had the great fortune to travel to the Galápagos with many University of Pennsylvania students past and present; seeing the archipelago through their eyes continually reminds me of the power and energy of this place. And every day, Deena, Brandon, and Melora show me why places like this one are worth saving. Brandon, *Giganotosaurus* never lived here, but this book is for you.

1

MANY LITTLE WORLDS:
THE GALÁPAGOS ENVIRONMENTS

LEFT: Male **FLOREANA LAVA LIZARD** sunning himself on a lava rock, Floreana Island

BELOW: Male **ESPAÑOLA LAVA LIZARD**, missing the end of his tail, sunning himself on Española Island

OPPOSITE:
GALÁPAGOS TORTOISE making its way through the mud in the highlands of Santa Cruz Island

PREVIOUS PAGE:
PACIFIC GREEN TURTLE heading back to the water after building her nest, Santiago Island

MANY LITTLE WORLDS:
The Galápagos Environments

In *The Voyage of the Beagle*, Charles Darwin called the Galápagos archipelago "a little world within itself." But it would be more accurate to see it as many worlds—a large set of unique habitats, or environmental *niches*, located together in a small place. This chapter presents a journey through them, beginning with the occasionally lush, but mostly inhospitable, terrain of these volcanic islands. These inland areas give way to the coastal zone, with its own complement of animals eking out an existence, which in turn transition down the water column to the shallow parts of the Pacific Ocean's floor.

ON LAND
On the surface, the Galápagos Islands look very different from the tropical paradise most visitors expect. These islands are volcanic in origin and relatively young, qualities that lead to many of their otherworldly features. Land-dwelling animals need to find a niche among the costal rocks, the scrubby plants just inland, or, on some islands, in the semi-tropical highlands.

Giant Tortoises may be the most easily recognized land-dwelling animals in the Galápagos, but they are far from the only ones. Lava lizards are widespread; there are nine species found throughout the islands. These lizards are an example of *adaptive radiation*, through which closely related but distinct species have evolved on different islands. The Galápagos is also home to three species of land iguanas, who live in the scrubby inland forests.

Male **GALÁPAGOS LAND IGUANA** feeding on vegetation, Santa Cruz Island

A relatively rare hybrid of the **GALÁPAGOS LAND IGUANA** and the **MARINE IGUANA**, South Plaza Island

OPPOSITE: A **GALÁPAGOS RACER** hunting, Bartolomé Island

A **GALÁPAGOS RACER** hunting for food. One of the few snakes found in the archipelago, this constrictor will eat insects, hatchlings, mice, rats, and even baby **MARINE IGUANAS**. Fernandina Island

MANY LITTLE WORLDS:
The Galápagos Environments

Visitors and scientists alike delight in observing Galápagos birds in their natural habitats. Darwin's observations of the Galápagos mockingbirds—which revealed the differences among the birds on different islands and between Galápagos and mainland mockingbirds—helped spark his evolutionary thinking.

GALÁPAGOS MOCKINGBIRD feeding on the fruit of a prickly pear cactus, Genovesa Island

OPPOSITE: **GALÁPAGOS DOVE** nesting on a prickly pear cactus, North Seymour Island

A closer look at the **CHILEAN FLAMINGO** (left) and the **GREATER FLAMINGO** (below), Floreana Island

OPPOSITE: Galápagos is home to the **GREATER FLAMINGO**. In this picture, a rare, itinerant **CHILEAN FLAMINGO** has joined the flock. Floreana Island

GREATER FLAMINGOS looking for food in a protected lagoon, Floreana Island

An elegant **WHITE-CHEEKED PINTAIL** duck swims in a shallow pond in the highlands of Santa Cruz Island

OPPOSITE: **WAVED ALBATROSS** jumping off a cliff, Española Island. These birds are so large that they need to be helped into the air by the wind

SHORT-EARED OWL seeking shelter from the rain, Genovesa Island

MANY LITTLE WORLDS:
The Galápagos Environments

AT WATER'S EDGE

The Galápagos marine environment begins where the coastal zone, or littoral zone, meets the ocean. Here, crabs and seabirds hunt for food, while iguanas sunbathe on the warm rocks. Here too, Pacific Green Turtles come out of the water to lay eggs; their babies face a harrowing journey to return to the sea after they hatch.

GHOST CRAB emerging from its hiding place in the sand to look for food, San Cristóbal Island

AMERICAN OYSTERCATCHER surrounded
by **SALLY LIGHTFOOT CRABS**, Santiago Island

After hatching, a baby **PACIFIC GREEN TURTLE** enters the
water for the first time at Urbina Bay, Isabela Island

Male **MARINE IGUANAS** heading out to sea to find food, Fernandina Island

MANY LITTLE WORLDS:
The Galápagos Environments

There is enormous activity in the shallow waters surrounding the islands. Bottlenose Dolphins surf and swim near crabs, sharks, penguins, and pelicans. Here visitors can also see the only seagoing lizard in the world, the Marine Iguana.

MARINE IGUANAS
swimming at the surface of the water, Sombrero Chino Island (left) and Isabela Island (below)

VELVET CRAB emerging from the shallow waters off Floreana Island

BOTTLENOSE DOLPHIN showing off for visitors off the bow of the *National Geographic Islander*, Floreana Island

BROWN PELICAN and **GALÁPAGOS SHARK** hunting the same school of fish, North Seymour Island

Mature (right) and immature (left)
GALÁPAGOS PENGUINS
swimming in Sombrero
Chino Bay

GALÁPAGOS PENGUIN curiously approaching the camera, Bartolomé Island

GALÁPAGOS PENGUIN swimming near the surface of the water, Sombrero Chino Island

MANY LITTLE WORLDS:
The Galápagos Environments

During their breeding season, the Marine Iguanas on Floreana and Española adopt breeding colors of bright red and green. Because of these colors, and because their breeding season happens around December, the Naturalist Guides call them "Christmas Iguanas."

MARINE IGUANAS
displaying breeding colors
and fighting for territory,
Española Island

OCTOPUS swimming in the waters off Santiago Island

ABOVE: **MEXICAN HOGFISH** challenging the camera, Sombrero Chino Island

MANY LITTLE WORLDS:
The Galápagos Environments

INTO THE OCEAN
Descending further into the ocean reveals yet another world. Shy octopuses dart in and out of their dens, searching for food and attracting mates. Schools of small fish swim together, while larger fish chase the smaller ones and even the humans who enter their domain. On the ocean floor, rays and sea stars make their homes among the sand and rocks.

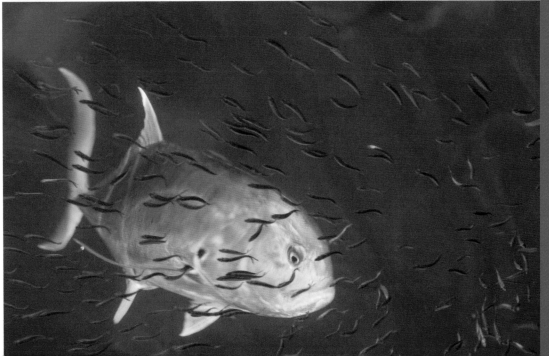

PACIFIC CREVALLE JACK chasing a school of smaller fish, off Baltra Island

DIAMOND STINGRAY nestling into the sand at the ocean floor, Gardner Islet

An extremely rare sighting of a **PYRAMID SEA STAR** with an extra arm, Champion Island

STONE SCORPIONFISH waiting to hunt, Champion Island

MANY LITTLE WORLDS:
The Galápagos Environments

The bottom of the ocean provides many opportunities for camouflage. By blending into their environment, or just by finding a good hiding spot, Galápagos animals can avoid threats from predators or wait for exactly the right moment to strike their prey.

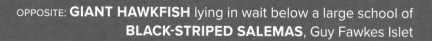
OPPOSITE: **GIANT HAWKFISH** lying in wait below a large school of
BLACK-STRIPED SALEMAS, Guy Fawkes Islet

FLAG CABRILLA positioning itself to catch
BLACK-STRIPED SALEMA, Santiago Island

GALÁPAGOS CONCH feeding on
algae, Bartolomé Island

Galápagos **BARNACLE BLENNY** emerging from its shell, off the coast of Santa Cruz Island

Three **PANAMAIC CUSHION STARS** with four, five, and six arms respectively. Off of Bartolomé Island

MANY LITTLE WORLDS:
The Galápagos Environments

EL NIÑO SOUTHERN OSCILLATION

Because life in the Galápagos is highly dependent on the ocean, these islands are sensitive to periodic changes in climate. One of the most dramatic such changes is the El Niño Southern Oscillation, more commonly referred to as "El Niño." What oscillates is the ocean temperature, which in turn has profound effects on both the weather and marine life. The water warms as the result of changing currents; during this period, much of the cold, nutrient-rich southern water does not reach the archipelago. This puts enormous stress on the red and green algae typically eaten by Marine Iguanas. While the changes to the weather during the 2015–2016 El Niño were not particularly noticeable on land, its effects were evident in observing the iguanas.

MARINE IGUANA eating algae in a typical year, Isabela Island

A **MARINE IGUANA** starving
due to lack of food during El Niño
2015–2016, Fernandina Island

Six months later, food was more
abundant than usual on Fernandina

OPPOSITE: At the end of the 2015–2016
El Niño, the cold, nutrient-rich water
returned, and the fish population
exploded. Santiago Island

A **DIAMOND STINGRAY** swims beneath **BLACK-STRIPED SALIMAS** at the conclusion of an El Niño year. Puerto Egas, Santiago Island

PACIFIC GREEN TURTLE eating lush algae at the conclusion of an El Niño cycle, off of Fernandina Island

2
FINDING FOOD

FINDING FOOD

Galápagos animals organize much of their lives around the search for food. Because there is so little food on these mostly barren islands, these animals display a remarkable set of adaptations for finding it. This chapter explores the behaviors of the hunters and the hunted, vegetarians, sand grazers, and food stealers. We will encounter underwater foragers who can excrete excess salt from seawater and omnivorous birds who drink the blood of baby sea turtles. But like so much in the Galápagos, our story of Galápagos animals finding food begins in the ocean.

Mature Galápagos Sea Lions survive by catching and eating fish. They forage over enormous distances, swimming six or more miles per day to find food. Other animals know sea lions are good at fishing, and some birds employ the strategy of trying to steal a meal from them.

PREVIOUS PAGE: **SALLY LIGHTFOOT CRAB** hunting an adult male **YELLOW WARBLER**, Urbina Bay, Isabela Island

GALÁPAGOS SEA LION catching and eating a fish in Tagus Cove, Isabela Island

GREAT BLUE HERON stealing a fish from a **GALÁPAGOS SEA LION**, Isabela Island

FINDING FOOD

Fishing isn't confined to mammals like the Galápagos Sea Lion. The remarkable Flightless Cormorant catches its prey by swimming, while the Brown Pelican plunge-dives, stunning its prey and then scooping it up in its beak.

BROWN PELICAN eating small fish just off Baltra Island

BELOW: **FLIGHTLESS CORMORANT** catching a **BARBERFISH,** off the coast of Isabela Island

FINDING FOOD

Many Galápagos animals live right at the water's edge, either catching their prey along the coast or venturing farther out to sea to find a meal. But not all animals who depend on food from the sea eat fish. For example, Marine Iguanas are vegetarians, foraging exclusively on algae underwater and along the coastline. They sneeze to excrete the excess salt they ingest by swallowing seawater. And sea predators themselves sometimes become food; Galápagos Hawks sometimes eat Galápagos Sea Lion and Galápagos Fur Seal carcasses, placentas, and pups.

LAVA HERON, a variety of **STRIATED HERON**, eating a catch of sardines, Fernandina Island

Juvenile **GALÁPAGOS HAWK** eating the flesh of a baby **GALÁPAGOS SEA LION**, Española Island

FINDING FOOD

Much of the Galápagos coastline is inhabited by the spectacularly colorful Sally Lightfoot Crab. These omnivores play an important role as recyclers in the ecosystem because they eat just about anything. But sometimes they themselves become food.

ABOVE: **SALLY LIGHTFOOT CRAB** eating a **SANTIAGO LAVA LIZARD**, Rabida Island

OPPOSITE: **ISABELA LAVA LIZARD** eating a **SALLY LIGHTFOOT CRAB**, Fernandina Island

YELLOW-CROWNED NIGHT HERON
eating a **SALLY LIGHTFOOT CRAB**,
Genovesa Island

FINDING FOOD

Pacific Green Turtles hatch from underground nests. The hatchlings race to the water but are often caught along the way, providing meals for hungry frigatebirds and other predators, such as pelicans, herons, and hawks.

MAGNIFICENT FRIGATEBIRDS frequently patrol the beaches for baby **PACIFIC GREEN TURTLES**. In these images, a **MAGNIFICENT FRIGATEBIRD** catches a hatchling on Santiago Island as it tries to make its way to the water

FINDING FOOD

One of the hardest animals to spot in the Galápagos is the aptly named Ghost Crab. These small crabs quickly disappear from view when they see potential predators or humans. They forage for small animals and particles of food on the beach by chewing up sand, separating and swallowing the food, and expelling the sand in tiny balls.

GHOST CRAB expelling sand balls, San Cristóbal Island

WAVED ALBATROSS feeding its chick with oil converted from digested food, Española Island

FINDING FOOD

One of the most dramatic ways of getting food is directly from the mouth of one's parents. Many Galápagos birds living near the water feed their chicks partially digested food.

While a WAVED ALBATROSS feeds its chick, an ESPAÑOLA MOCKINGBIRD attempts to steal the food. Española Island

SWALLOW-TAILED GULL feeding regurgitated
squid to its chick, Genovesa Island

FINDING FOOD

Like all mammals, Galápagos Fur Seal and Galápagos Sea Lion pups rely on their mother's milk in the first years of life.

OPPOSITE: **GALÁPAGOS FUR SEAL** nursing, Santiago Island

BELOW: Juvenile **GALÁPAGOS SEA LION** suckling, Española Island. Although this individual is missing both hind flippers, he survived for several years after this picture was taken.

FINDING FOOD

While many Galápagos animals are reliant in some way on the ocean for their food, not all are. The remarkable Hummingbird Moth resembles a hummingbird in behavior and appearance, hovering in the air as it gathers nectar from flowering plants.

ABOVE, BELOW AND OPPOSITE: **HUMMINGBIRD MOTH**
gathering nectar from Galápagos Shore Petunia, Rabida Island

FINDING FOOD

The four species of Galápagos
mockingbird are opportunistic feeders,
eating many different plants and animals,
and even drinking blood.

SAN CRISTÓBAL MOCKINGBIRD eating the fruit of a Muyuyo plant, San Cristóbal Island

GALÁPAGOS MOCKINGBIRD eating prickly pear cactus fruit, Genovesa Island

GALÁPAGOS MOCKINGBIRD eating a **SANTIAGO LAVA LIZARD**, Rabida Island

ESPAÑOLA MOCKINGBIRD eating a baby **PACIFIC GREEN TURTLE** on the beach at Gardner Bay, Española Island

FINDING FOOD

Small Galápagos birds feed on insects, fruit, and seeds. Flycatchers, Yellow Warblers, and Lava Herons eat insects, while the different species of Galápagos finches each specialize in eating a different kind of food.

ABOVE: **VERMILLION FLYCATCHER** eating an insect, Rabida Island

GALÁPAGOS FLYCATCHER eating a moth on Floreana Island

LAVA HERON eating a **LARGE PAINTED LOCUST**, Santiago Island

BELOW: Male **YELLOW WARBLER** eating a fly onboard the *National Geographic Islander*

FINDING FOOD

There are very few mammal species in the Galápagos, where most niches typically occupied by mammals are occupied by reptiles or birds. The endemic Santa Fé Rice Rat is one exception. Most active after dark, it feeds on vegetation, seeds, and small invertebrates.

SANTA FÉ RICE RAT eating vegetation, Santa Fé Island

Like the **SANTA FÉ RICE RAT**, the **GALÁPAGOS LAND IGUANA** is also a vegetarian. Conditions were so dry on the day this picture was taken that the iguana climbed a prickly pear cactus looking for food. North Seymour Island

FINDING FOOD

Aquatic foraging in the Galápagos is not confined to the coast. Brackish lagoons are a source of aquatic insects and larvae for Flamingos and Black-necked Stilts.

GREATER FLAMINGOS filter-feeding in a lagoon, Rabida Island

BLACK-NECKED STILT searching for aquatic invertebrates in a brackish lagoon, Santa Cruz Island

FINDING FOOD

Great Blue Herons, Galápagos Hawks, and owls are top predators, and they have extremely varied diets. They prey on lava lizards, Marine Iguanas, insects, shellfish, and sometimes even small birds and mammals.

GREAT BLUE HERON catching a female **ESPAÑOLA LAVA LIZARD**, Española Island

GALÁPAGOS HAWK eating goat meat bait
from a National Park study, Santiago Island

BELOW: **GALÁPAGOS HAWK** catching a **MARINE IGUANA**, Fernandina Island

FINDING FOOD

Why find your own food when you can steal it? Frigatebirds are kleptoparasites, often stealing food from other birds rather than hunting.

BLUE-FOOTED BOOBY feeding its youngster, with a male frigatebird swooping in to steal the food, North Seymour Island

OPPOSITE: **SHORT-EARED OWL** eating a **GALÁPAGOS DOVE**, Genovesa Island

GREAT FRIGATEBIRD stealing food from a **NAZCA BOOBY** feeding its chick, Genovesa Island

FINDING FOOD

Perhaps the most spectacular and dramatic way to find food in the Galápagos is by plunge-diving or "dive-bombing." The Blue-footed Booby flies over the ocean looking for fish, then it tucks its wings in, plunges into the water, and catches fish under the water.

BLUE-FOOTED BOOBY dive-bombing at Espumilla Beach, Santiago Island

BLUE-FOOTED BOOBIES dive-bombing off the coast of Isabela Island

A **BLUE-FOOTED BOOBY** has just caught a fish under water, off the bow of the *National Geographic Endeavour*

3

ICONS OF THE GALÁPAGOS:
TORTOISES, MOCKINGBIRDS, FINCHES, AND BOOBIES

ICONS OF THE GALÁPAGOS:
Tortoises, Mockingbirds, Finches, and Boobies

Although this book is primarily organized by types of habitats and behaviors, several animal species or groups are so iconic and representative of the Galápagos that they call out for special recognition: Galápagos Tortoises, mockingbirds, finches, and boobies. Beyond being visually striking, each of these types of animal has played an important role in shaping evolutionary theory, both in Darwin's time and in our own.

GIANT TORTOISES

The Galápagos Tortoises are perhaps the most iconic of Galápagos animals. Widespread among many of the islands, these massive grazing reptiles fill many of the same niches that herbivorous mammals fill on the mainland. Depending on their source of food, Galápagos Tortoise *carapaces* (the upper part of the shell) are said to be dome-shaped, saddleback-shaped, or intermediate in shape. Domed tortoises have rounded carapaces, shaped something like a helmet. The scales around their necks (the *cervical* scales) are pointed forward and downward, giving them easy access to food on the ground.

PREVIOUS PAGE: Dome-shaped **GALÁPAGOS TORTOISES**, resting in a freshwater pond in the highlands of Santa Cruz Island

Male dome-shaped **GALÁPAGOS TORTOISE** in the highlands of Santa Cruz Island

Domed **GALÁPAGOS TORTOISE** drinking, highlands of Santa Cruz Island

ICONS OF THE GALÁPAGOS:
Tortoises, Mockingbirds, Finches, and Boobies

In some environments, however, the only available food is up on the trunks and limbs of trees or cactuses, and these tortoises cannot reach it. But tortoises whose cervical scales are tilted a little higher are able to reach their necks upward, allowing them to access this food. Over many generations, natural selection in these environments has favored tortoises with upward-tilting cervical scales, leading to the evolution of saddleback tortoises, whose carapaces are shaped a bit like a horse's saddle.

Lonesome George, the last tortoise from Pinta Island, died in 2012. Here he is seen in his enclosure at the Charles Darwin Foundation, Santa Cruz Island

ICONS OF THE GALÁPAGOS:
Tortoises, Mockingbirds,
Finches, and Boobies

There are different theories about the shape of the first tortoises that arrived in the Galápagos. Did they all arrive with the same type of carapace, or were different founding populations shaped differently? One common view is that all of the tortoises were dome-shaped when they arrived, but that, as the population spread out to different islands and to different locations within the larger islands, they began to adapt to their local environments.

Large male domed **GALÁPAGOS TORTOISE** eating grass and other vegetation during a rainstorm, highlands of Santa Cruz Island

OPPOSITE: Intermediate-shaped **GALÁPAGOS TORTOISE** chewing and swallowing vegetation, San Cristóbal Island

Diego, a saddleback **GALÁPAGOS TORTOISE** from Española Island, can reach his neck very high up. Charles Darwin Research Station, Santa Cruz Island

ICONS OF THE GALÁPAGOS:
Tortoises, Mockingbirds,
Finches, and Boobies

MOCKINGBIRDS

The four species of mockingbirds certainly leave an impression on visitors to the Galápagos. The Galápagos Mockingbird, the most widespread species, is highly inquisitive and will often approach humans. The Española Mockingbird is genuinely fearless, often pecking at the legs of visitors or anywhere else it can get a drop of moisture. The Floreana Mockingbird and the San Cristóbal Mockingbird are much shyer; bird-watchers need patience to spot one.

Mockingbirds are what "first thoroughly aroused" Darwin's attention about the distribution of species on the archipelago, according to his book *The Voyage of the Beagle*. At first, he simply noticed that the mockingbirds in the Galápagos Islands differed from those from mainland South America. Later, he came to appreciate that the mockingbirds on different islands looked different from one another. How could islands so close together have similar birds with different morphologies? Darwin came to see this as what we now call *adaptive radiation*, in which natural selection shapes different populations of the same type of animal to the particular environments in which they live.

FLOREANA MOCKINGBIRD on Champion Island

SAN CRISTÓBAL MOCKINGBIRD on San Cristóbal Island

GALÁPAGOS MOCKINGBIRD on Rabida Island

ICONS OF THE GALÁPAGOS:
Tortoises, Mockingbirds,
Finches, and Boobies

FINCHES

For many people, the Galápagos is synonymous with Darwin's finches—the species of ground, tree, and warbler finches that are part of the subfamily Geospizinae. Although Darwin himself did not at first appreciate their significance, they represent a remarkable instance of adaptive radiation and are frequently used as an example of the phenomenon in biology textbooks. The most significant differences among the finches are in their beak size and shape. These differences allow them to eat different kinds of food: small soft seeds, large hard seeds, insects buried in the bark of trees, and so forth. They have also provided scientists with one of the most detailed studies of evolution in action. Over 40 years, scientists Rosemary and Peter Grant have closely observed the Medium Ground Finch and the Cactus Finch of Daphne Major Island, showing how changing climatic conditions led to small changes in the size and shape of the beaks of these birds.

Male and female **SMALL TREE FINCHES** displaying full breeding plumage, highlands of Santa Cruz Island

Baby **SMALL GROUND FINCH** in its nest, Punta Pitt, San Cristóbal Island

Male **LARGE GROUND FINCH** eating *Tribulus* seeds, Genovesa Island

OPPOSITE: Leucistic **SMALL GROUND FINCH**, highlands of Santa Cruz Island

Female **MEDIUM GROUND FINCH** eating bark from a Palo Santo tree, Santa Cruz Island

Female **MEDIUM GROUND FINCH** nesting in a prickly pear cactus, Santa Cruz Island

GREY WARBLER FINCH standing on a coral beach, Genovesa Island

Male **COMMON CACTUS FINCH**, Santa Cruz Island

LARGE CACTUS FINCH feeding on prickly pear cactus fruits, with a **SHARP-BEAKED GROUND FINCH** waiting for his chance to feed, Genovesa Island. New evidence suggests that these Genovesa finches may be sufficiently isolated from their cousins on other islands to be counted as separate species—the **GENOVESA CACTUS FINCH** and **GENOVESA GROUND FINCH**, respectively

ICONS OF THE GALÁPAGOS:
Tortoises, Mockingbirds,
Finches, and Boobies

BOOBIES

Unlike Galápagos Tortoises, finches, and mockingbirds, boobies are not endemic to the Galápagos; they are found in other places. But like the other animals, they display a remarkable set of behavioral adaptations that are particularly evident in the Galápagos. Blue-footed Boobies live in flat open areas, and they fish by diving into the water near the coastline. Red-footed Boobies nest in the branches of trees and fish far offshore. And Nazca Boobies live on cliffs and fish in areas between the islands.

BLUE-FOOTED BOOBY parents and babies at Punta Pitt, San Cristóbal Island

A very rare observation of a **BLUE-FOOTED BOOBY** with three eggs (they normally lay two), Punta Pitt, San Cristóbal Island

An even rarer observation: three **BLUE-FOOTED BOOBY** chicks in the same nest, Punta Pitt, San Cristóbal Island. Walter has encountered three chicks being raised together only one time in his 12 years observing wildlife in the Galápagos

RED-FOOTED BOOBY couple showing brown and white color variants, Genovesa Island

RED-FOOTED BOOBY preparing to land on a branch, Punta Pitt, San Cristóbal Island

Baby **RED-FOOTED BOOBY** begging for food, Punta Pitt, San Cristóbal Island

ABOVE AND OPPOSITE: Immature **RED-FOOTED BOOBIES** preparing for fledging, Genovesa Island

OPPOSITE: **NAZCA BOOBY** landing with nesting material, Española Island

NAZCA BOOBIES courting in front of the "blowhole," a fissure in the lava where water soars 300 feet in the air, Punta Suarez, Española Island

Immature **NAZCA BOOBY** exploring the ocean
between Fernandina and Isabela Islands

4

COURTSHIP, MATING, AND BIRTH

COURTSHIP, MATING, AND BIRTH

From an evolutionary point of view, nothing is more critical than finding a mate, having offspring, and ensuring that those offspring can survive to reproduce. To this most important of activities, Galápagos animals devote enormous time and effort. For some species, courtship and mating have evolved into elaborate rituals involving song, dance, and the exchange of gifts. Others meticulously prepare nests—in the trees, on the rocks, or under the beach—for sheltering their young. For many species, parental care is freely given, sometimes over many years. But for a few unusual species, parental care is just as easily revoked, sentencing offspring to certain death.

Galápagos mating rituals can be quite elaborate. Swallow-tailed Gulls pair-bond and build nesting platforms out of pieces of coral. Boobies sing, dance, and exchange gifts prior to mating. And the rare Flightless Cormorants engage in a beautiful, synchronized courtship dance both before and after mating.

SWALLOW-TAILED GULLS engaging in a courtship ritual, Española Island

PREVIOUS PAGE: **SALLY LIGHTFOOT CRABS** mating, Española Island

OPPOSITE: Male **NAZCA BOOBY** offering nesting material as a gift to a female, Española Island

BLUE-FOOTED BOOBY offering nest material to attract a mate, North Seymour Island

BLUE-FOOTED BOOBIES engaging in a courtship dance, North Seymour Island

FLIGHTLESS CORMORANTS engaging in a courtship dance, which continues after mating, Fernandina Island

SMOOTHTAIL MOBULA jumping out of the water. The jumping behavior is not well-understood, but it may be a pre-mating ritual.
Between Santiago and Rabida Islands

YELLOW-CROWNED NIGHT HERONS engage in a pre-mating ritual. Santiago Island

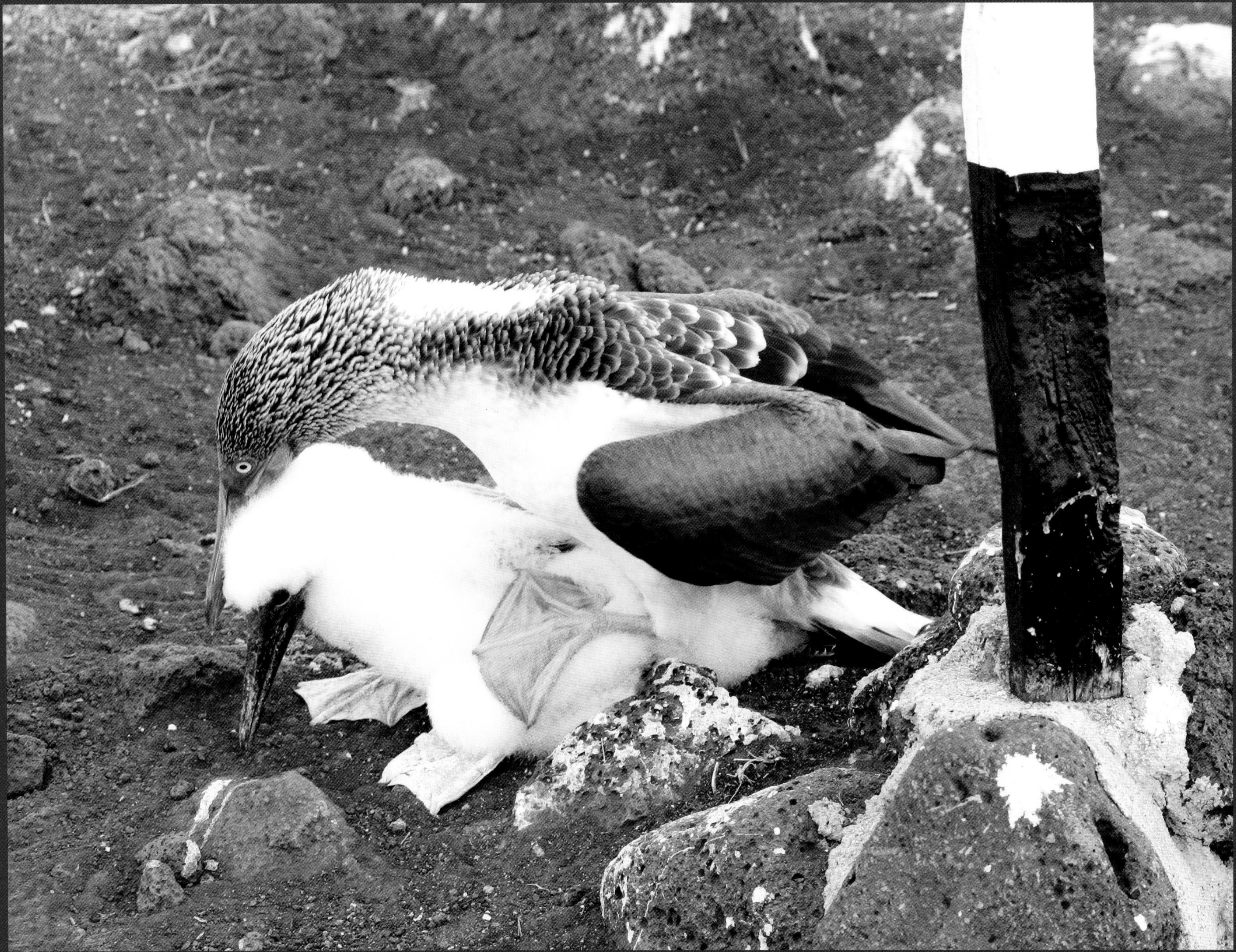

OPPOSITE: Extremely rare observation of an adult male **BLUE-FOOTED BOOBY** mounting a juvenile, North Seymour Island

PACIFIC GREEN TURTLES mating on a beach, Floreana Island

COURTSHIP, MATING, AND BIRTH

Other Galápagos animals engage in little courtship, if any.

GALÁPAGOS TORTOISES mating, Santa Cruz highlands

MARINE IGUANAS mating, Fernandina Island

COURTSHIP, MATING, AND BIRTH

The birds and reptiles of the Galápagos employ many strategies to protect their eggs and their offspring. Some birds build nests in trees, others on bare rocks. Some nests are built out of leaves and twigs, others out of bits of coral and urchin spikes, and still others are simply large holes under the beach. Once they lay eggs, some parents, like Blue-footed Boobies, keep a close watch on them. Others, like Pacific Green Turtles, leave the eggs and offspring to fend for themselves.

Male **YELLOW WARBLER** preparing a nest, Santa Cruz Island

SWALLOW-TAILED GULL collecting fragments of coral to use as nesting material, Genovesa Island

Male **MAGNIFICENT FRIGATEBIRD** carrying nesting material, North Seymour Island

GALÁPAGOS MOCKINGBIRD collecting nesting material, Santiago Island

RED-FOOTED BOOBY carrying a branch back to its nest, Genovesa Island

"Battle of the Sticks": A male **GREAT FRIGATEBIRD** trying to steal nesting material from a **RED-FOOTED BOOBY**, Genovesa Island

RED-FOOTED BOOBIES building a nest, Genovesa Island

This male **FLIGHTLESS CORMORANT** is carrying seaweed to build a nest. After mating, male Flightless Cormorants bring seaweed, sea stars, twigs, and other materials to their mates, who immediately begin building a nest. Fernandina Island

PACIFIC GREEN TURTLE
covering eggs in her under-
beach nest, Santiago Island

ABOVE AND OPPOSITE: **PACIFIC GREEN TURTLE** babies emerging from the nest and making their way out to sea, Bartolomé Island

A **GALÁPAGOS HAWK** watches a **PACIFIC GREEN TURTLE** return to the ocean after laying her eggs. Espumilla Beach, Santiago Island

COURTSHIP, MATING, AND BIRTH

Some Galápagos animals, like the Pacific Green Turtle and the Marine Iguana, leave their babies to fend for themselves. But for other Galápagos animals, after a new baby is born, the work is just beginning. Baby animals need to be fed, groomed, taught, and protected from predators.

WAVED ALBATROSS
preening a chick,
Española Island

RED-FOOTED BOOBY preening a chick, Genovesa Island

WAVED ALBATROSS parents preening a newborn
chick together, Española Island

Mother **GALÁPAGOS SEA LION** carrying her pup to a safer location, North Seymour Island

OPPOSITE: Mother holding a newborn **GALÁPAGOS SEA LION**, with its placenta and umbilical cord still visible, North Seymour Island

OPPOSITE: Adult female **GALÁPAGOS SEA LION** returning to her pup after fishing. Female sea lions recognize their pups by call. Santiago Island

Unusual sight of a **GALÁPAGOS SEA LION** nursing two pups, Española Island

NAZCA BOOBY feeding its chick, Española Island

NAZCA BOOBY feeds its first chick; the other will hatch in a few hours. Española Island

Male **BLUE-FOOTED BOOBY** feeding his chick, North Seymour Island

A pair of **BLUE-FOOTED BOOBIES** grooming each other while caring for a newborn chick and an unhatched egg, Punta Pitt, San Cristóbal Island

AMERICAN OYSTERCATCHER bringing part of a **SALLY LIGHTFOOT CRAB** to a juvenile, Santiago Island

SEA LION pup learning by playing and interacting with its mother, Champion Island

COURTSHIP, MATING, AND BIRTH

One of the most unusual behaviors seen in the Galápagos is *siblicide*. Blue-footed Boobies and Nazca Boobies lay two eggs a few days apart. If the first chick survives and the second hatches, a Blue-footed Booby chick may eject its nest mate from the nest while the parent watches. For Nazca Boobies, this ejection is *obligate*; it happens every time. The ejected chick will quickly die either from lack of food, the hot tropical sun, or predation. No one is sure why boobies engage in siblicide, but a widely accepted hypothesis holds that the second egg is an insurance policy. In the harsh climate of the Galápagos, resources are too scarce to support two chicks, but they also make counting on the viability of a single egg risky. This hypothesis proposes that natural selection has favored populations who try to raise only a single chick, but lay two eggs as insurance.

BLUE-FOOTED BOOBY chick sleeping next to its sibling's egg, North Seymour Island

NAZCA BOOBY sleeping next to its sibling's egg, Española Island

This sequence shows the older **BLUE-FOOTED BOOBY** chick pushing its younger sibling away from the nest while the mother looks on, North Seymour Island

NAZCA BOOBY pushing its sibling out of nest while its parent watches, Genovesa Island

5

GALÁPAGOS ANIMALS INTERACTING

GALÁPAGOS ANIMALS INTERACTING

Galápagos animals strive to cope with their harsh environment. This often means struggling to find food when it is scarce, hiding from predators, and finding a mate. But much of the life of an animal involves dealing with other animals. Sometimes it is necessary to fight, but sometimes play is welcome. Some animals depend on each other through various cooperative *mutualisms*, while other curious animals keep a careful eye on the humans who have recently arrived in their environments. Animals are intimately part of each other's environments, and no examination of animal behavior would be complete without understanding these relationships.

PREVIOUS PAGE: **BLUE-FOOTED BOOBIES, MAGNIFICENT FRIGATEBIRDS, BROWN PELICANS, BROWN NODDY** terns, and **GALÁPAGOS SHARKS** engaging in a feeding frenzy on the same school of **ANCHOVIES,** off of Baltra Island

A female **GALÁPAGOS SEA LION** struggles ashore after being attacked by a shark, Española Island

GALÁPAGOS ANIMALS INTERACTING

One of the most dramatic interactions among Galápagos animals is fighting—for territory, access to mates, or food. Iguanas are territorial and fight to protect their territory, and their mating success is tied to the quality of the territory they hold.

Male **MARINE IGUANAS** fighting over territory and access to females, Puerto Egas, Santiago Island

Male **GALÁPAGOS LAND IGUANAS** fighting over territory and access to females, Santa Cruz Island

GALÁPAGOS ANIMALS INTERACTING

Many instances of fighting ultimately are about mating. Although Waved Albatrosses form mating pairs, additional copulation is common and often a source of skirmishes. Similarly, large male Galápagos Sea Lions will protect their beaches for weeks at a time, preventing other males from gaining sexual access to females.

Male **WAVED ALBATROSS** approaching a mating couple who fights back, Española Island

GALÁPAGOS ANIMALS INTERACTING

In the most barren and dry parts of the Galápagos, access to preferred nesting and feeding grounds can mean the difference between successfully raising offspring or not. There are often spirited disagreements over who can lay their eggs and who can feed in a given location.

OPPOSITE: Although they patrol a beach for weeks at a time, alpha male **GALÁPAGOS SEA LIONS** eventually have to leave the beach to get food. After hunting, a large male rushes back to the beach to chase a younger male away, Española Island

Alpha male **GALÁPAGOS SEA LION** patrolling his beach, Fernandina Island

Male **PACIFIC GREEN TURTLES** fighting for access to females. Tagus Cove, Isabela Island

GALÁPAGOS SEA LION playing with a **PACIFIC GREEN TURTLE**. Punta Vincente Roca, Isabela Island

BROWN NODDY terns fighting over nesting ground, Fernandina Island

Showdown between a group of **ESPAÑOLA MOCKINGBIRDS** protecting their feeding ground and a group of newcomers, Gardner Bay, Española Island

Male **GALÁPAGOS FUR SEALS** fighting over territory, Santiago Island

Young **GALÁPAGOS HAWKS** play-fighting with a stick, Fernandina Island

GALÁPAGOS ANIMALS INTERACTING

Not every interaction between animals is brutal. Galápagos animals play with members of their own species, with other animals, and even with plants and sticks.

OPPOSITE: Juvenile **GALÁPAGOS SEA LION** playing with the fruit of a prickly pear cactus, Champion Island

Sometimes sea lions make risky choices about their playmates. This juvenile **GALÁPAGOS SEA LION** was playing with a **TIGER SNAKE EEL**, which eventually got stuck in his nostril. San Cristóbal Island

This playful juvenile **GALÁPAGOS SEA LION** is using a **RED-LIPPED BATFISH** as a toy, perhaps practicing his fishing skills. Champion Island

Juvenile **GALÁPAGOS SEA LION** playing with a **BULLSEYE PUFFER**.
Cerró Dragon, Santa Cruz Island

GALÁPAGOS ANIMALS INTERACTING

Other interactions between animals provide mutual benefit, what biologists call *mutualism*. Animals depend on one another for help in finding food, finding shelter, and keeping clean.

A male **YELLOW WARBLER** approaching a **GALÁPAGOS SEA LION** to catch flies, San Cristóbal Island

Female **GALÁPAGOS LAVA LIZARD** catching flies while perched on the head of a **MARINE IGUANA**, Fernandina Island

OPPOSITE: In a land of spectacular sights, seeing a **BLUE WHALE** still leaves one speechless. To the right of the blowhole, a remora, or suckerfish, feeds on the leftovers of the whale's food. Tagus Cove, Isabela Island

In the foreground, **SALLY LIGHTFOOT CRABS** protect themselves against the rough sea. In the background, the *National Geographic Islander* sails past. Puerto Egas, Santiago Island

GALÁPAGOS ANIMALS INTERACTING

Although humans are newcomers to the Galápagos, for better and for worse they have left an indelible mark on its landscape. The archipelago is under intensive pressure from rising interest in tourism and a growing local population. But humans are now part of the Galápagos story and illustrate new types of animal interactions.

FLIGHTLESS CORMORANT putting on a display of drying its wings for the guests of the *National Geographic Endeavor*, Fernandina Island

Posing for the camera, or just unconcerned with the presence of a human, a group of immature **RED-FOOTED BOOBIES** preparing for fledging, Genovese Island

PACIFIC GREEN TURTLE covering her nest after laying her eggs,
Las Bachas Beach, Santa Cruz Island

This curious **GALÁPAGOS FLYCATCHER** is about to land on a
visitor's camera lens. Santiago Island

OPPOSITE: A **YELLOWTAIL DAMSELFISH** approaches the camera. These fish are also known as "farmers" because they protect their feeding ground. Off of Santiago Island

This **GALÁPAGOS SEA LION** has snatched an iPhone from a tourist. The sea lion repeatedly swam up to the small boat to show off the phone, then dove down with it. After about 30 minutes, Walter managed to rescue the phone. Off of Floreana Island

Seemingly oblivious to where he has landed, a male **FLIGHTLESS CORMORANT** engages in a courtship display on the back of a snorkeler. Tagus Cove, Isabela Island

GALÁPAGOS SEA LION curiously approaching a video camera,
North Seymour Island

SANTA FÉ RICE RAT looking for food in a hiker's backpack,
Santa Fé Island

Two symbols of San Cristóbal Island together: *León Dormido* (Kicker Rock) and a **GALÁPAGOS SEA LION** on a *panga* (inflatable dinghy), San Cristóbal Island

OPPOSITE: **BLUE-FOOTED BOOBIES** plunge-diving for fish while tourists look on, Santiago Island

OPPOSITE: A **GALÁPAGOS MOCKINGBIRD** grabs a visitor's shoelace. Cerró Dragon, Santa Cruz Island

ESPAÑOLA MOCKINGBIRD, curious about the new arrivals in its environment, lands on Walter's head. Punta Suárez, Española Island

CONCLUSION

Visitors to the Galápagos often ask their guides "What's your favorite animal?" or "What's your favorite island?"

In a land of such riches, these may be impossible questions to answer. Each island and every animal has an incredible story to tell. From penguins living at the equator, to vegetarian iguanas that forage for food underwater, to the only species of cormorant that doesn't fly, each population illustrates ecological relationships in dramatic ways. Each population also raises deep questions about the evolutionary forces that have shaped this place: Why is a hawk the top predator? Why are the biggest land grazers reptiles? How can three species of boobies live in almost exactly the same place without competing for food? Each species has much to teach us. Each is special and unique. Each is a favorite.

GALÁPAGOS PENGUIN in the process of molting, Santiago Island

OPPOSITE:
BLUE-FOOTED BOOBIES
dive-bombing, Bolivar channel between Fernandina and Isabela Islands

GREATER FLAMINGO in a brackish lagoon during the rainy season. Punta Comorant, Floreana Island

SPECIES INDEX

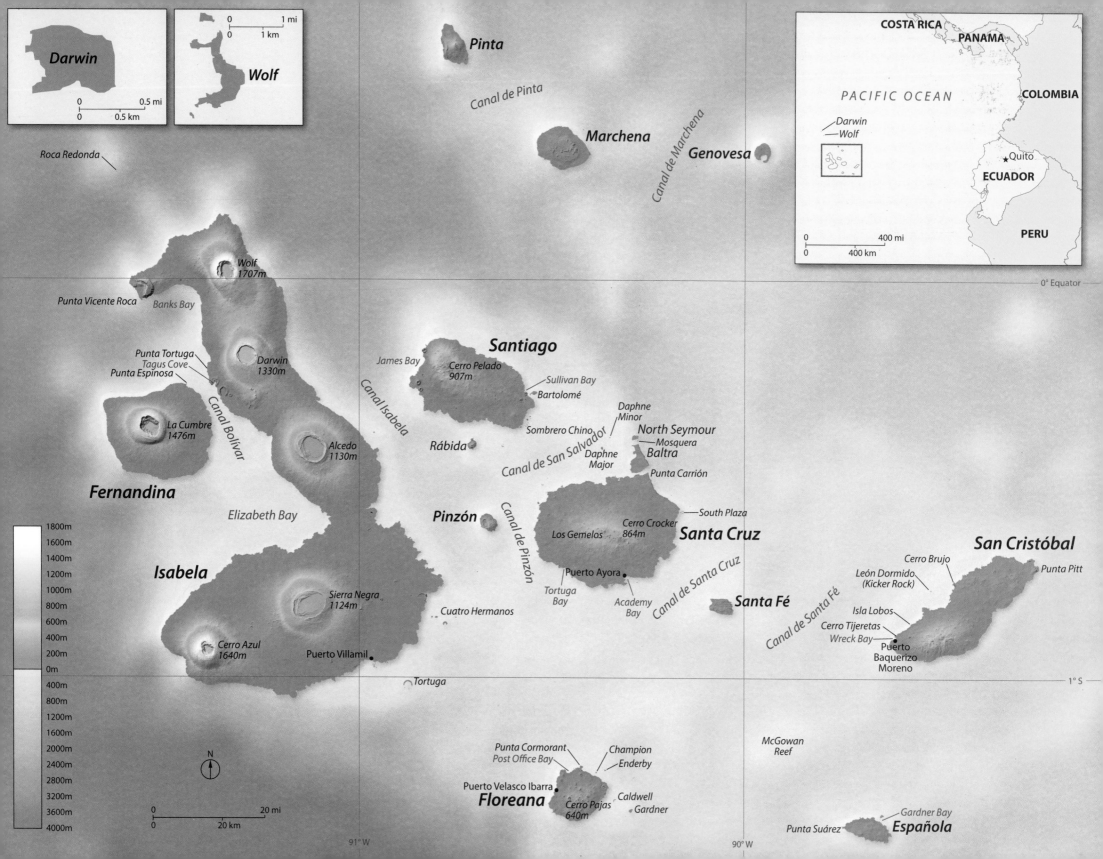

Darwin

0 — 0.5 mi
0 — 0.5 km

Wolf

0 — 1 mi
0 — 1 km

COSTA RICA
PANAMA
COLOMBIA

PACIFIC OCEAN

Darwin
Wolf

Quito ★
ECUADOR

PERU

0 — 400 mi
0 — 400 km

Pinta

Canal de Pinta

Roca Redonda

Marchena

Genovesa

Canal de Marchena

Wolf
1707m

0° Equator

Punta Vicente Roca   *Banks Bay*

Santiago

James Bay

Cerro Pelado
907m

Sullivan Bay
Bartolomé

Punta Tortuga
Tagus Cove
Punta Espinosa

Darwin
1330m

Daphne Minor

North Seymour
Mosquera
Baltra

La Cumbre
1476m

Canal Bolívar

Alcedo
1130m

Canal Isabela

Sombrero Chino

Rábida

Daphne Major

Punta Carrión

Fernandina

Canal de San Salvador

South Plaza

Pinzón

Cerro Crocker
864m

Elizabeth Bay

Los Gemelos

Santa Cruz

San Cristóbal

Cerro Brujo

Punta Pitt

1800m
1600m
1400m
1200m
1000m
800m
600m
400m
200m
0m

Isabela

Sierra Negra
1124m

Canal de Pinzón

Puerto Ayora

Tortuga Bay

Academy Bay

Canal de Santa Cruz

Santa Fé

Canal de Santa Fé

León Dormido
(Kicker Rock)

Isla Lobos

Cerro Tijeretas
Wreck Bay

Cerro Azul
1640m

Cuatro Hermanos

Puerto Villamil

Puerto Baquerizo Moreno

400m
800m
1200m
1600m
2000m
2400m
2800m
3200m
3600m
4000m

Tortuga

1° S

N

McGowan Reef

Punta Cormorant
Post Office Bay

Champion
Enderby

0 — 20 mi
0 — 20 km

Puerto Velasco Ibarra

Floreana

Cerro Pajas
640m

Caldwell
Gardner

Gardner Bay

Punta Suárez   **Española**

91° W

90° W